AQÜITÍN

ENVIRONMENTAL EDUCATIVE MAGAZINE

OF WATER AND NATURE FOR CHILDREN

No 4

AUTHOR AND TRANSLATER: YOLANDA MA. JORGE BESTEIRO

ILLUSTRATOR: ADOLFO LÓPEZ MEJÍA

1

Topics: **WATER AND CLIMATE CHANGE.**

No 1-Curiosities about planet earth. "The Water Footprint Did you know that?

No 2-Know the place where you live... Climate Change, curiosities of the Incas.

No 3- Recommendations for the reduction of greenhouse gas emissions.

No.4- Aqüitín's famous phrases.

No.5-Relato Los Castores del Elba.

No.6-Familiarize yourself with" Aqüitín's concepts.

No.7- Topics about water and biodiversity.

No.8 Learn more about the greenhouse effect.

There is nothing better than educating to build a better world for all".

Section 1.

Curiosities about planet earth. The Water Footprint

Did you know that 70% of the planet Earth is covered by water?

Of this water, 97% is in the oceans in the form of salt water, and the remaining 3% is in the glaciers in the form of ice, and only less than 1% is consumable water, approximately 160 million km3, although not all of it is available for living beings. For a part corresponding to 10% is 750 meters below the surface of the earth, and 2000 m3 per year are safe from contamination or deterioration with saline water.

Although we are mentioning many numbers, I want you to keep the main idea that the percentage of useful water available for living beings is very small, so that if we do not take care of water, waste it or pollute it, we will be walking towards the failure and death of humanity in the not-too-distant future.

What is water?

We all know what it is, but could we define it?

Water is a molecule formed by two hydrogen atoms and one oxygen atom.

And what is a molecule?

It is the smallest particle that makes up a substance, and has the physical and chemical characteristics and properties of the substance.

The atoms that form the molecules can be the same as those of oxygen, which has two equal atoms of oxygen O2, or different, as in the case of the water molecule, which has two hydrogen atoms and one oxygen atom forming its molecule.

Did you know that... Water is the best solvent that exists, in it substances are transported within the human body and we are not only talking about food, also chemical compounds within cells and tissues, and all living things need water, both animals and plants.

To all this, we must add that without water life is not possible, we can be without food for several days, but it is not possible to survive or have good health without drinking water, in addition, water is not only used as a drink, but also in the industrial sectors, agricultural sectors, energy and domestic uses. Therefore, it is essential to make a rational use of water, so that it is efficiently used to the maximum without wasting it.

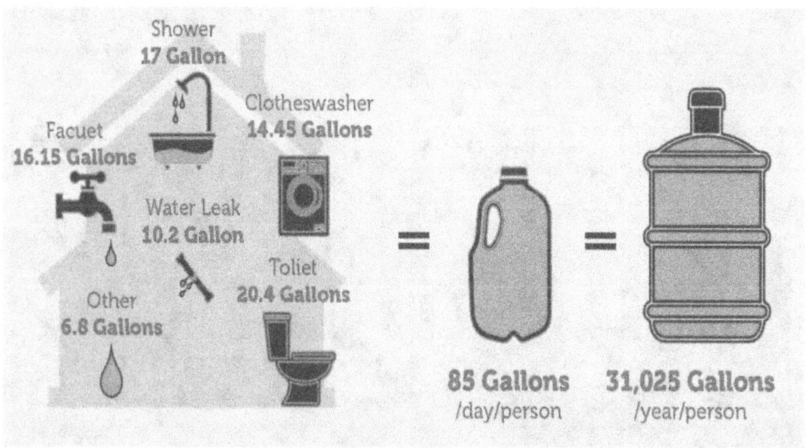

The water footprint is the term used to refer to the total amount of water used by humans.

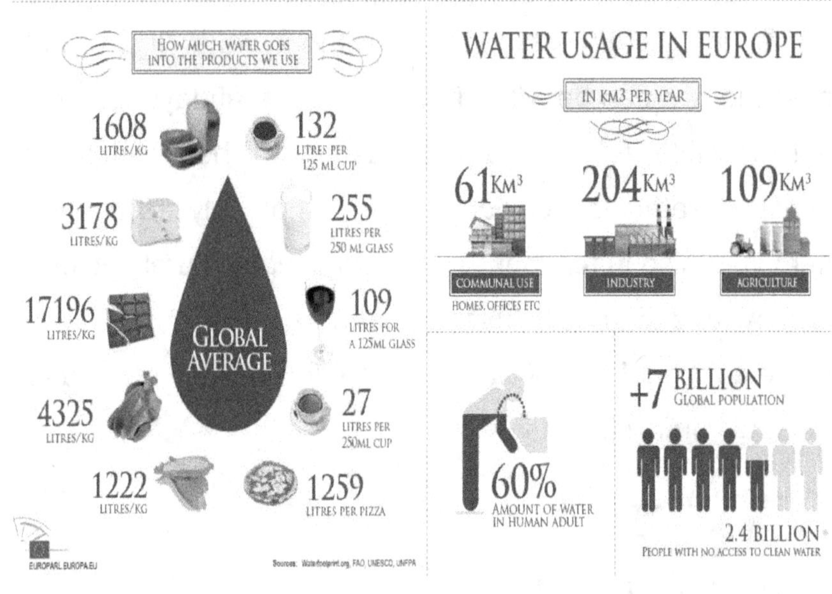

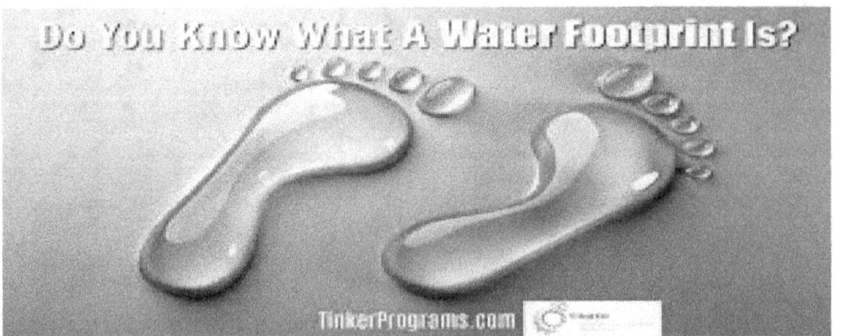

The water footprint measures the amount of water used to produce each of the goods and services we use. It can be measured for a single process, such as growing rice, for a product, such as a pair of jeans, for the fuel we put in our car, or for an entire multi-national company. The water footprint can also tell us how much water is being consumed by a particular country – or globally – in a specific river basin or from an aquifer

Our body contains 70 percent water.

Some of the functions of water in living beings:

- It favors the maintenance of adequate body temperature of the body in humans and animals.
- It is indispensable for the realization of photosynthesis in plants, in which, in addition to obtaining energy, it fixes CO_2 and releases O_2. And this released O_2 is one of the

greatest contributions of O2 in the earth's crust, necessary for the life of humans and animals on earth.

- It constitutes the habitat of infinite aquatic and marine species.

All of the above animals are found in freshwater habitats. (Clockwise from top-left: American alligator, rainbow trout, bullfrog, river otter)

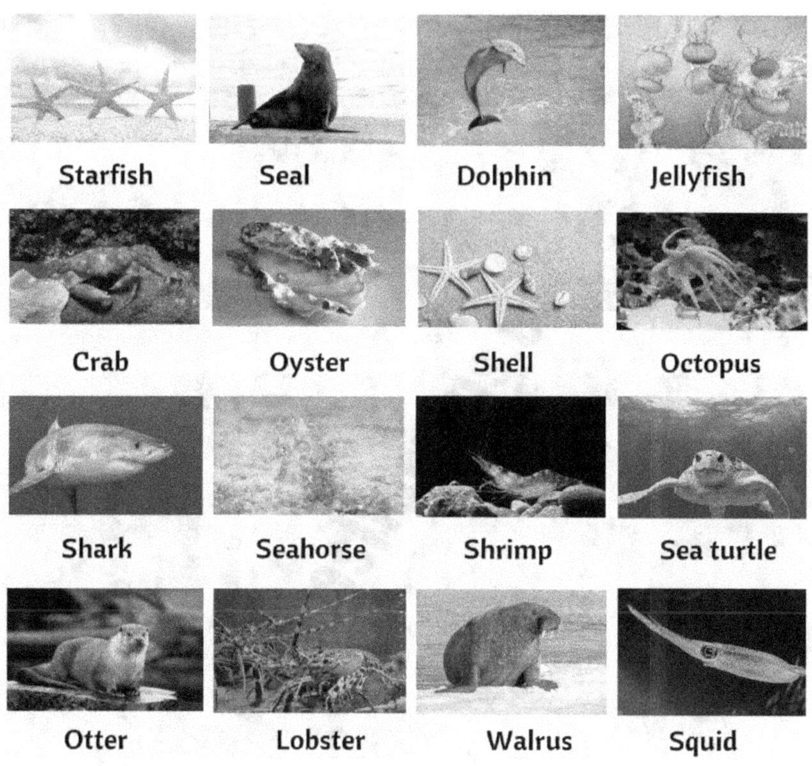

Starfish	Seal	Dolphin	Jellyfish
Crab	Oyster	Shell	Octopus
Shark	Seahorse	Shrimp	Sea turtle
Otter	Lobster	Walrus	Squid

Ocean animals.

The plants need water too.

Terrestrial animals

Values of water consumption of farm animals in liters per day.

Drinking water is a human right.

Do you think humans and land animals can consume salt water for drinking if we cannot find fresh water?

No, we don't. If we consume it, we will dehydrate and die.

The technology to desalinate water and make it potable or at least of a minimum quality suitable for human consumption or use in irrigation areas for agricultural crops is also expensive.

Rain and snowfall recycle 500 billion m3 per year, but ¾ of this precipitation (37.5 billion m3) falls into the saline oceans and seas, although 1.25 billion m3 per year falls on land."

It is important for you to know that we can help prevent the massive evaporation of water from the earth's surface and how?

By planting large areas of forests, reforesting. The opposite of what man does, because the indiscriminate felling of trees destroys ecosystems and habitats of many animals, in addition to favoring the loss of soil quality and the leakage of water into the atmosphere.

And add to all this, how complex and costly is the management and distribution of water for human consumption, the cost of bringing water to urban and metropolitan areas to where we live.

It is not fair that more than 663 million people do not have drinking water near their homes, and that more than 842 thousand deaths each year are due to the consumption of unsafe water combined with lack of hygiene.

About 1.8 billion people in the world use water contaminated with fecal matter as drinking water and can contract diseases such as dysentery, cholera, typhoid and polio. And as an additional fact that manifests the disaster, we know that more than 80% of wastewater, return to the ecosystem without being treated. What a disaster!

New concepts:

Sublimation is the process of changing from the solid state to the gaseous state without passing through the liquid state. ... The reverse process, that is, the direct passage from the gaseous state to the solid state, is called reverse sublimation or desublimation.

A spring is the natural source of water and not the water that gushes out of the ground or between rocks. It may be permanent or temporary. It originates in the seepage of water, rain or snow, which penetrates an area and emerges in another of lower altitude.

Below, you can see very well all the paths that water can follow on earth, the hydrological cycle of water. Some of them we will not deal with in this edition of the magazine because they are more specialized content, but others we do know and have talked about before and you can work on them with the teachers in class: Precipitation, evaporation, condensation, sublimation, runoff or runoff, stored groundwater, spring.

<u>Water Cicle</u>

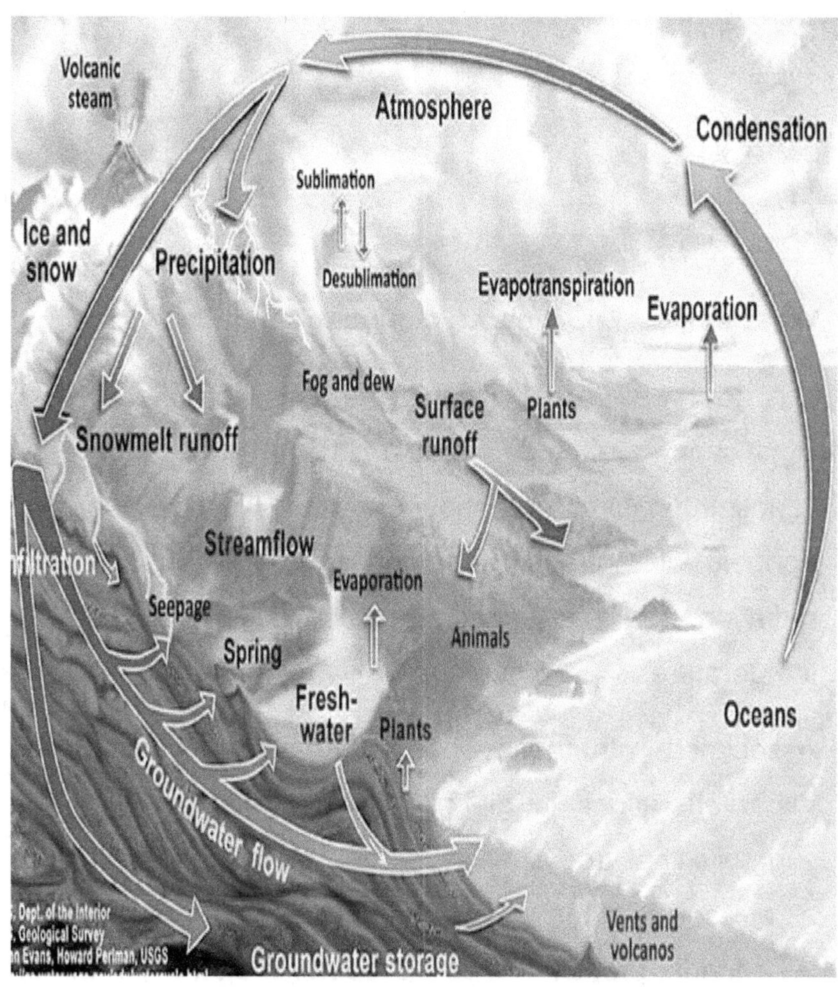

Section 2 Learn and know the environment in which we live.

What do you know about climate change?....

It is now a scientific fact that the global climate is being significantly altered as a result of increasing concentrations of greenhouse gases. These gases are trapping an increasing portion of the Earth's infrared radiation and are expected to increase the planetary temperature.

Associated with these potential changes, there will be major alterations in global ecosystems. Scientific work suggests that tree species ranges may vary significantly as a result of global climate change. For example, studies in Canada project losses of approximately 170 million hectares of forest in southern Canada and gains of 70 million hectares in northern Canada, so global climate change would imply a net loss of 100 million hectares of forest, and these are just some of the global changes that await us.

Did you know that nearly 200 million people are at risk of being displaced by 2050 because climate change could cause sea level rise, freshwater shortages and reduced agricultural capacity in some regions of the world.

Climate change poses a direct threat to children's ability to survive, grow and thrive. UNICEF 2021.

Extreme weather events such as cyclones and heat waves, which are becoming more frequent and intense, endanger children's lives and threaten to destroy infrastructure essential to their well-being.

Floods put water supply and sanitation facilities at risk, favoring the emergence of diseases such as cholera, to which children are particularly vulnerable.

The people least responsible for climate change are children, yet they will suffer the worst consequences.

Did you know...the ten hottest years since 1980?

-The three gases directly responsible for climate change are carbon dioxide, nitrous oxide and methane, which are responsible for global warming caused by burning fossil fuels. During the last century the level of carbon dioxide in the atmosphere has increased by 25%, nitrous oxide by 19% and methane by 100%.

-Didn't you know. The average temperature of the earth's surface has risen between 0.3 and 0.6 degrees Celsius and by the year 2100 it could be 3.5 degrees Celsius and the melting of the polar ice caps and glaciers could cause a rise in sea level of up to one meter by the year 2100. Entire nations could be submerged.

We humans are the only ones responsible for the disaster. It is incredible, but despite the fact that emissions of these gases should be reduced by 50 and 70%, they are increasing.

From our magazine we are aware that unfortunately we cannot do anything to change the sad reality that is coming because it is a fact, but we can slow down and reduce its effects. Although the outcome is disastrous for the entire planet, it will be even more unjust for those who will bear the brunt, the poor of the earth, when the consequences become evident.

Some consequences in the Americas:

The indigenous populations of the Americas who live off their rivers and who have contributed so much to contemporary civilization may disappear from the face of the earth.

We can learn from our ancestors:

Let us remember that the Inca culture showed us how much they had learned from nature with their hydraulic works.

The hydraulic works of today should take notes of the great hydraulic works that nature makes at no cost, as in the case of waterfalls, where the water that falls from so high is purified by the oxygen in the air as it falls, so that when the water reaches the ground it is completely clean of impurities, ready to drink.

In ancient times the Indians of America, particularly those belonging to the vast Inca empire, worked wonders observing nature in order to obtain water supplies and use it in agriculture.

The survival of the entire empire depended on this and their great economic and social development and success was largely due to the rational and intelligent use of the knowledge acquired from nature and its implementation.

Many techniques used today such as wells, dams and canals that include the collection, transmission, reservoir and distribution of water from rivers, lakes or rain, for the use of man and domestic animals, as well as for the irrigation of agricultural land were used by this great people hundreds of years ago.

Curiosities

The first known hydraulic dam in Mexico, the Mequitongo dam, located in the valley of Tehuacan, seems to have been built in 700 BC.

The area covered by this dam has been calculated at 2.38 hectares and the volume of water retained at about 37,000 cubic meters. So, we often believe that we far surpass the wisdom of the Indians, but nothing could be further from the truth when it comes to water, we should learn from them.

Inca Empire.

In the valley of Teotihuacan, in 100 B.C. there was a system of canals, both for irrigation and rainwater control.

The construction of dams was another of the hydraulic works most used by the Incas to divert the waters of the rivers and to take advantage of the water conducted through canals, in lands located on the banks of the riverbeds.

In the 700s of our era, the Xiquila aqueduct was built in the area of Tehuacan, with great mathematical knowledge to develop a platform or terrace where to place the channel and thus achieve the required slope.

All these pre-Hispanic hydraulic engineering works allowed for better crop yields. With their wisdom, the Incas were able to supply fresh water to their people and their agriculture, and at the same time, prevent soil erosion. It is precisely the latter that, even today with the agricultural economic development that we have, we are not able to avoid.

The terraces are one of the best engineering works that the Incas bequeathed us, this marvel of their ingenuity allows better use of water from different levels of height and fall staggered to be more efficient staggered with a better use by crops of this water and dragging minerals in its gentle fall, also avoiding flooding at surface level, which drown the plants.

Lack of irrigation		Overwatering

We already know that water is indispensable for life, but the excess of it can also be harmful for many crops.

In the following image we can appreciate the mastery in the design of a terrace made by the Incas. The mastery of the Incas did not stop there, they also made complex drainage, both in the coastal valleys and in the mountains to protect crops from torrential rains and flooding.

Terraces Incas

The Incas indians also built artificial hollows or depressions, called cochas, which were opened in the ground to accumulate rainwater in the highland areas. A cocha is very similar to what we know today as reservoirs, where water is stored for when it is needed.

Cocha Inca.

Section 3. Recommendations for the reduction of greenhouse gas emissions.

In order to explain in depth what greenhouse gases are, we must first go to the root and explain what they are. Greenhouse gases are those gases that accumulate in the Earth's atmosphere and absorb infrared energy from the Sun. This creates the so-called greenhouse effect, which contributes to global warming.

But why is it important to understand what greenhouse gases are?

Mainly because human action has been crucial in their development. Therefore, we need to understand what actions emit them in order to reduce their harmful effect on the Earth.

The Industrial Revolution was the beginning of a whole series of changes in the industrial fabric that have triggered CO_2 emissions. Man's role in increasing CO_2 emissions prevented this gas from being released naturally, as happens in volcanic eruptions or even forest fires.

But there are other greenhouse gases. Some of them have a natural origin and others are the result of human activity and are, like CO2, harmful to the environment. Here are the most important ones.

The main greenhouse gases

Water vapor. It arises as a result of evaporation. The amount of water vapor in the atmosphere depends on the temperature of the ocean surface. Most of it originates as a result of natural evaporation, in which man's action does not intervene.

Carbon dioxide (CO2). If we ask what the greenhouse gases are, CO2 is the first that comes to mind. Of the greenhouse gases, this is the most important because it is the one most associated with human activities, and the main responsible for this effect. Its concentration in the atmosphere is due to the use of fossil fuels for industrial processes and means of transportation. Its emission comes from combustion processes (oil, coal, wood) or from volcanic eruptions or forest fires.

Methane (CH4). Its origin lies in fermentations produced by specialized anaerobic bacteria found in swampy areas, crops such as rice and in emissions from the intestinal tract of livestock. It is also produced by leaks from natural reservoirs and industrial pipelines.

Nitrous oxide (N2O). A greenhouse gas caused mainly by the massive use of nitrogen fertilizers in intensive agriculture. It is also produced by other sources such as thermal power plants, automobile exhausts and aircraft engines, biomass burning, and the manufacture of nylon and nitric acid.

Chlorofluorocarbons (CFCs). These are man-made chemical compounds that are present in small concentrations in the atmosphere but are extremely potent in the greenhouse effect they cause.

They have multiple industrial uses in refrigeration systems, as components of aerosols, aluminum production and electrical insulators, among others.

Tropospheric ozone (O3). Also caused by the burning of polluting energy sources.

The United Nations Framework Convention on Climate Change (FCCC) was signed at the World Summit in 1992 by 162 governments.

This summit, which is currently in force in 2021, focused on stabilizing greenhouse gases in the atmosphere, which would prevent dangerous anthropogenic interference in the climate system.

In the United Kingdom, a program was established to achieve this goal by promoting the efficient use of energy as a means of reducing carbon dioxide generation in all sectors of that nation.

In electricity generation, investment has been made in combined heat and power plants, which use heat energy that was previously lost.

In the domestic sector, this will be achieved through improvements in the thermal insulation of homes and improved efficiency of household appliances through better design and better use, as in the case of lighting.

Public transport, through improvements in engine technology, better engine maintenance, compliance with speed limits and more discreet use of acceleration and braking.

For this to be implemented, it is necessary to invest in education and information campaigns.

<u>**Specific measures include:**</u>

- Improve the efficiency of automobiles. This would be achieved through better technology, lightening the structure, improvements in engines and transmissions, reducing aerodynamic friction, reducing wheel resistance, etc.
- Accelerate energy efficiency improvements in industries, residences, and commercial and public establishments through effective policies.
- Stimulate and accelerate research and development of technologies based on renewable energy sources.
- End deforestation and stimulate reforestation.

Windmills that generate wind energy.

Sección 4

Frases célebres de Aqüitín.

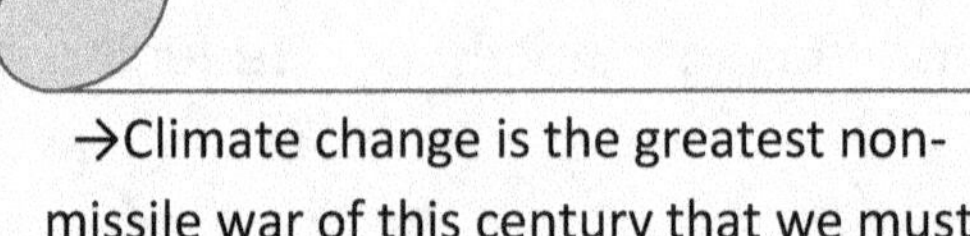

→Climate change is the greatest non-missile war of this century that we must face.

→The greatest injustice on earth is the thirst of a child when there is so much water.

→Drought is like the sadness that ages the soul when love is lacking.

→America, cradle of civilizations, master of Water Engineering.

→The color of the cracked earth is the reflection of Childhood without lights.

→Water is life itself, love is the peace of the earth.

From Aqüitín we want to tell all children and young people not to be intimidated by all the catastrophes generated by man until today.

Children are not responsible for these things, but they will receive the consequences anyway, so from our magazine we invite you not to stand idly by.

Learn, be informed of what is happening around you, know the environmental problems of your city, town or village, and in general of the planet because you are learning that it belongs to everyone, and what happens in one place on earth ends up affecting us all, no matter how distant the others are from the place of the affectation.

It is necessary to be informed, to know what to do in each case, it is not enough to know what or where it happened, you have to say what you think, expose your opinions, demand that the rulers of your town and country make responsible decisions.

Denounce, correct, suggest, but you need to gain knowledge to do this in the best way.

Ask yourself questions about everything around you and become actively aware of this issue that affects all living beings, not just humans.

If we manage to motivate you enough to start thinking about all this, and make it part of your reality and routine, we are satisfied in our magazine. Because today you are a boy or a girl, but you will be a good woman and a good man in the future. And you have to start now.

There is no turning back for nature and for many forms of life in the oceans, rivers, forests, jungles, grasslands, etc. that no longer have anything to do for their young, but you can make a difference by becoming aware and not letting it happen anymore, from your small environment to far beyond. ¡**START NOW!**

You owe it to yourself and to everyone. Don't look the other way when you see injustice of any kind. Don't allow it, from a small animal being mistreated, to a forest on fire, garbage being thrown away, oil being dumped instead of recycled, plastics being thrown into the sea, water being wasted.

With these simple examples I show you that you can do a lot.

From AQÜITÍN

WE PREPARE ENVIRONMENTAL CHAMPIONS, NATURALISTS.

DEFENDERS OF ANIMALS, PLANTS AND NATURE AS A WHOLE.

DEFENDERS OF THE PLANET.

 **"The Beavers of the Elbe".**

A couple of young beavers fled to the marshy banks of the Elbe River in search of better luck. Stalked by numerous enemies, they came to a place that seemed quiet and with plenty of alternative food. The frightened couple were among the few survivors of their family who managed to escape.

When they rested a little, they began to build their fortress and commented among themselves that later, in the highest and steepest part, they would also make some tunnels to take refuge. They had to be always alert, in case they had to go out suddenly and hide if they were threatened by some unforeseen danger.

The little house had become authentic, they made it with pieces of sticks and dry branches brought here and there by the beaver from the river bank and that he waterproofed with mud, earth and reeds. Its interior was very cozy, it had several chambers and the entrance was always covered by water.

The beaver family is really amazing, they learn these arts from their parents who teach them that if the water level drops too low, they have to cut down trees with their powerful teeth and quickly build a dam to dam it.

These creatures only need to live on a riverbank to build their castles and to feed on soft bark plants, preferring willows and poplars, and they supplement their diet with grasses. Many of the grasses grow in the reeds, so they are not very selective in this respect, however, although they are satisfied with little, if they do not have peace of mind they cannot live.

Their enemies multiplied everywhere, the otters were their closest enemies, but not the only ones, many besieged the beavers and since ancient times their ancestors were victims of persecution, their meat was considered a delicious dish, their skin was highly prized and their fleshy and oval tails were used to make delicacies and to top it all off, even their fat was said to be magic medicine.

The poor beavers had no way out, wherever they went they were lost, death was their prey. Of all the predators that exist, they had the worst of them as their enemy, man.

Nearby, an old and hermit fisherman had settled down, who, embittered by his bad luck, his character turned sour, so he decided to isolate himself from all his peers. Centurion, as the fisherman was called, had been mistreated since he was a child. Since he had been orphaned when he was only eight years old, the poor man lived on what he managed to catch with his own skills and by running errands for the locals. To make matters worse, the villagers took advantage of the boy, demanding major tasks that the little boy could barely do. Then they paid him with pittances, which were only enough to put a little food in his mouth at night.

Fortunately for the young Centurion, time passed quickly and as he became a man, luck smiled on him and he met a good woman. But as time did not make his character improve and he was so bitter, the noble Centurion preferred not to make her suffer any more. Finally, she had nothing to do with his pitiful former life and was only trying to make him happy. The man, believing that his unfortunate luck could make her unhappy too, because he thought that his misfortune was contagious to anyone who came near him, decided to walk away.

Centurion was not so old, only with the unkempt beard that always accompanied him, he looked like an old man, the sun of the sea had tanned his skin and strengthened the wrinkles and together with the sadness that approached him, his hair had turned gray.

The shack that Centurion had built for himself was only a few meters from the fortress of the beaver couple who had already noticed his presence in the place, but it was mating season and the young rodents were too busy to notice the intruder.

In the mornings, the fisherman would go fishing downstream and return as the sun set, so that by nightfall he would drop like a stone.

Spring had come to the banks of the Elbe and with it, all the shoots were greening up, the fish were returning to their native regions and Centurion had no choice but to sit on the riverbank casting lots to see if anything would fall into his nets, perhaps a straggling minnow.

A couple of young beavers fled to the marshy banks of the Elbe River in search of better luck. Stalked by numerous enemies, they came to a place that seemed quiet and with plenty of alternative food. The frightened couple were among the few survivors of their family who managed to escape.

When they rested a little, they began to build their fortress and commented among themselves that later, in the highest and steepest part, they would also make some tunnels to take refuge. They had to be always alert, in case they had to go out suddenly and hide if they were threatened by some unforeseen danger.

The little house had been made with pieces of sticks and dry branches brought here and there by the beaver from the river bank, which he waterproofed with mud, earth and reeds. Its interior was very cozy, it had several chambers and the entrance was always covered by water.

The beaver family is really amazing, they learn these arts from their parents who teach them that if the water level drops too low, they have to cut down trees with their powerful teeth and quickly build a dam to dam it.

These creatures only need to live on a riverbank to build their castles and to feed on soft bark plants, preferring willows and poplars, and they supplement their diet with grasses. Many of the grasses grow in the reeds, so they are not very selective in this respect, however, although they are satisfied with little, if they do not have peace of mind they cannot live.

Their enemies multiplied everywhere, the otters were their closest enemies, but not the only ones, many besieged the beavers and since ancient times their ancestors were victims of persecution, their meat was considered a delicious dish, their skin was highly prized and their fleshy and oval tails were used to make delicacies and to top it all off, even their fat was said to be magic medicine. The poor beavers had no way out, wherever they went they were lost, death was their prey. Of all the predators that exist, they had the worst of them as their enemy, man.

Hours and hours passed and the sun went down, it was then when, disappointed and with his eyes lost, he thought he saw movement under the water.

His astonishment was extreme, it was beavers swimming so close to him, playing and frolicking, two plump little beavers were jumping in and out of the clean water.

The poor man was hungry, he had been sitting there for hours without catching anything, however, those little animals filled his guts with excitement and he couldn't stop squirming. He did not know for sure what to do, but he preferred to spend a few more minutes contemplating such beauty.

Before the beginning of spring, the beaver had given birth to two little ones, who, now more agile and strong, were daringly learning to dive with dexterity into the water.

Centurion had never seen beavers in that area and the impressive scene of the playful little ones, as if they were children, moved him deeply, bringing back his best childhood memories, when his mother was still alive and gave him so much affection.

It was incredible, the humble man thought quietly, how nature gave strength to her children and offered them her favors. Centurion was amazed at the things he saw the curious creatures doing. They behaved like human beings.

As he looked around, he noticed that the water level had dropped and that very close to the beavers was a pair of adult beavers that were surely their parents. The adults seemed very busy moving small logs with their paws and mouths, their movements were fascinating and the skill with which they were damming excited him.

That must have been why the usual fish had moved away, now he understood many things.

The creatures he watched in amazement had a prodigious natural intelligence. Without noticing the time, the night caught him and he could see a beautiful dam finished, which, if he had not seen it made with his own eyes, he would never believe that it was made by such builders.

Centurion had discovered feelings unknown to him which had hitherto been denied him, nobility, kindness, and his heart grew so large within his breast that he could not fit within himself. The beaver family was worthy of living in that place, they deserved a chance and he was there to give it to them.

So, he set his mind to it and in a prudent time that he hardly noticed, since his life had changed so much that he wanted to make up for all the time he had lost. The scenes he witnessed gave his life a radical turn, gave him a sense of meaning, which made him want to start all over again and give himself hope, he wanted to be useful doing something that would make him feel proud of himself.

Several autumns, winters and springs passed before that beautiful place welcomed dozens of beavers that made the central part of the Elbe River their own.

Thus, the fisherman contributed to the adaptation of these important and curious creatures of nature, preventing them from disappearing for good. Fortunately for the species, some connoisseurs of these animals carried out several campaigns years later, moving them to other more favored zones, which today constitute protected areas.

The beaver family was very happy in Centurion's company. The fisherman returned to the village in search of his wife who was still waiting for him and they reconciled and he also surrounded himself with children and grandchildren who made him very happy.

His life changed radically and he became a great connoisseur of these creatures and everyone in the area consulted him about them. He even wrote a book about their life forms, which is currently a source of study for many naturalists. In homage to the anonymous lovers and defenders of nature.

Beavers lived in the Czech section of the Elbe until the 18th century when they were exterminated by man. The last beaver was seen in 1722 on the outskirts of the town of Decín, located on the banks of the Elbe near the German border.

In 2001 a small outpost of beavers crossed the Czech-German border and appeared on the stretch of the Elbe between the towns of Ústí and Decín in North Bohemia.

Elbe River in Germany

THE END

Section .6-Familiarize yourself with Aqüitin concepts.

Create concepts with Aqüitin, noting the way it clarifies and defines.

Concepts according to Aqüitin:

Drought: Water scarcity in which we are all involved and which is a symbol of misery and death in third world countries.

Aqüinostalgia: A feeling of longing that overwhelms Aqüitin when he remembers his childhood in what once were the springs.

Resume: Natural occurrences of good health that water experienced before human intervention.

Greenhouse effect: Man-made catastrophic phenomenon, in which some toxic gases accumulate in the Earth's atmosphere and absorb infrared energy from the Sun, causing global warming of the planet.

Technology: Word used by engineers in their inventions, which do nothing more than copy and decipher the intelligence of nature.

Incas: Indian empire that donated its great wisdom in engineering to the Inca Empire.

Climate change: Natural disaster of global warming caused by man.

Drainage: Ancient Inca technique, very useful today, used to protect crops from rains and floods.

Geosphere: Refers to soils.

Biosphere: Includes living plants and animals.

Anthropogenic: concept that defines man's activity that does not include his fateful contribution to nature.

Hydrosphere: Layer of the earth made up of the planet's waters.

Atmosphere: layer of air surrounding the earth.

Anthroposphere: the geographical and social environment in which human life and activity takes place.

In the natural sciences, the earth is composed of five layers, each with a medium and a component that characterizes them. For example, the. The geosphere, through the soils.

Man's relationship with the rest of the environmental spheres has caused his impact to modify the pre-existing environments or layers.

It is said that since the 21st century, virgin nature is almost impossible to distinguish. At least in large areas.

Man has modified almost in its entirety what was known as the biosphere.

Section 7.-Themes on water and biodiversity.

For centuries, European rivers have been used as a source of drinking water, food and irrigation, as well as for domestic and industrial waste disposal, energy production, transportation, recreation and tourism.

Generations of humans have altered the rivers and used their biological richness and fertile floodplains as the basis of our economy.

The way we now use and manage rivers and the marshy areas associated with their floodplains is causing environmental damage across the continent. Most of the threats come directly from human influence:

Hydroelectric schemes, dam construction, waste dumping, intensification of agriculture, deforestation, urbanization, dredging, engineering works and river course variation are some of the human actions on nature that only contribute by their mismanagement to making things worse.

These actions have diminished the economic, recreational and cultural value of the river. The scale and cost of the repairs needed to restore living rivers is steadily increasing. Many species of invertebrates, mammals, birds and amphibians that depend on river systems for their survival have been depleted in large parts of Europe.

If we add to all this the very serious consequences that the effects of climate change will cause.

What will happen to so many species of animals and plants?

Scientists using simulation models were able to predict the following effects on the atmosphere by greenhouse gases and to a lesser degree on atmospheric aerosols.

<u>**Conclusions from these models**</u>:

- average global warming of between 1.5 and 4.5 °C .(grade centigrade).

- The stratosphere will cool significantly.

- Surface shivering will be greater at high latitudes in winter, but less during the summer.

- Global precipitation will increase by 3 to 15%.

- There will be a year-round increase in precipitation in the high latitudes, while some tropical areas will experience small decreases.

According to the International Union for Conservation of Nature (IUCN), eleven European fish species are in danger of extinction.

In Spain, the sturgeon disappeared due to poor water quality and the construction of a dam in Alcalá del Río (Seville). In addition, in 1932, a famous caviar factory was established on the banks of the Guadalquivir, which caused overfishing of this fish.

Like the sturgeon, many others may cease to live if we do not act soon. Restoration projects are an important step to save them; but first, we must learn to love the rivers.

It is clear that the forecast of impending climate change disaster ahead is very close to what is actually happening now.

Before addressing the topic of climate change, it is very important to establish the differences between weather and climate.

Weather: refers specifically to the determination of the behavior and evolution of the processes that govern the atmosphere in the following hours (generally 12, 24, 48 and 72 hours).

Climate: related to the concept of permanence and in this sense deals with the analysis of atmospheric processes around their average values.

The average values are the result of the evaluation of observations over long periods of time, generally not less than 30 years.

It is also defined as the fluctuating set of atmospheric conditions, which is characterized by the states and evolutions of the weather in a given place or region or in the entire planet, during a relatively long period of time.

Although basically the climatic variables are related to the atmosphere, the predominant atmospheric processes in a place or region are related to the earth's surface, including the continental and oceanic crust and part of the upper mantle (lithosphere), the oceans, inland seas, rivers and groundwater (hydrosphere) and the land areas covered by ice (cryosphere).

There is also a close relationship between these processes and the vegetation and other living systems of both the continent and the ocean (biosphere and anthrosphere).

Since climate is generally related to the prevailing conditions in the atmosphere, it is described on the basis of atmospheric variables such as temperature and precipitation, called climatic elements; however, it could also be identified with the variables of other components of the climate system.

Throughout history, climate fluctuations have occurred on time scales ranging from years (interannual climate variability) to millennia (global climate changes). These variations have been caused by changes in the way the different components of the climate system interact and in the forcing factors.

Section 8 Learn more.

What are greenhouse gases (GHG)?

Greenhouse gases are naturally occurring and anthropogenic (emitted by human activity) gases whose presence contributes to the greenhouse effect.

Why is it important to understand what greenhouse gases are? And the main greenhouse gases:

Mainly because human action has been crucial in their development. Therefore, we need to understand what actions emit them in order to reduce their harmful effect on the Earth.

What is CO2?

It is a gas released by humans and many animals when they breathe, it is the air that comes out of our nose. It is also called carbon dioxide.

But it is also in the atmosphere the same as Oxygen O2 and other gases, produced in the atmosphere.

And if we explain it more, we will say that CO2 is a molecule formed by one atom of carbon and two atoms of oxygen.

CONSEQUENCES OF THE GREENHOUSE EFFECT

The increase in the earth's average temperature brings with it the modification of living conditions on the planet.

Melting ice will cause sea levels to rise and release more methane, among other consequences.

Melting of glacier masses

The retreat of glaciers also has its own consequences: the reduction of the albedo - the percentage of solar radiation that the earth's surface reflects or returns to the atmosphere -, the global rise in sea level or the release of large plumes of methane are just a few, and all of them are dramatic for the planet.

Flooding of islands and coastal cities.

Polar bears and many other animals living at the poles are dying for lack of food, as much of their food is found in the ice-covered depths. According to the Intergovernmental Panel on Climate Change (IPCC), during the period 1901-2010 the global average sea level rose by 19 centimeters.

It is estimated that by the year 2100 the sea level will be between 15 and 90 centimeters higher than it is today and will threaten 92 million people.

Humans, especially coastal populations and those living near rivers and beaches, will have a big problem.

More devastating hurricanes

The intensification of the greenhouse effect does not cause these extreme weather events, but it does increase their intensity.

The formation of hurricanes is related to sea temperature-they only form over waters with a temperature of at least 26.51 degrees Celsius (C).

Species migrations

Many animal species will be forced to migrate in order to survive the variations in the main climatic patterns altered by the progressive increase in temperatures.

Humans will also have to move: according to the World Bank, the number of people forced to flee their lands due to extreme droughts or violent floods could reach 140 million by 2050.

Desertification of fertile areas

Global warming has a profound impact on soil degradation processes and favors the desertification of areas of the planet, a phenomenon that destroys all the biological potential of the affected regions, turning them into barren and unproductive lands.

Impact on agriculture and livestock farming

Global warming has already altered the length of the growing season in large parts of the planet.

Similarly, variations in temperatures and seasons influence the proliferation of insects, invasive weeds and diseases that could affect crops.

The same is true for livestock:

Climate variations directly affect major species in multiple ways: reproduction, metabolism, health, etc.

CONSEQUENCES OF THE GREENHOUSE EFFECT ON HUMAN HEALTH

The greenhouse effect also directly affects human health through:

Food shortages.

The Food and Agriculture Organization of the United Nations (FAO) states that climate change will affect the availability of food: in its latest biennial report on the state of food and agriculture, it warns that a decline in agricultural production will lead to food shortages, most severely affecting sub-Saharan Africa and South Asia.

The spread of diseases and pandemics.

In addition to the problems arising directly from pollution, the World Health Organization (WHO) states that global warming will cause infectious diseases such as malaria, cholera and dengue fever to spread to many more areas of the planet. Extreme heat will increase and aggravate cardiovascular and respiratory problems.

The decline in crop and livestock production will lead to food shortages.

HOW CAN THE CONSEQUENCES OF THE GREENHOUSE EFFECT BE SOLVED?

WITH SOLUTIONS THAT INTEGRATE HUMANS; ANIMALS AND NATURE.

SOME PROPOSALS:

-Reducing the emission of so-called greenhouse gases - such as CO2 or CH4 - is not the only solution to curb the greenhouse effect.

-Replace plastic bags with bags made of recyclable natural materials.

-Use renewable energies.

Use public transport and other non-polluting means, such as cars or electric bicycles.

-Promote ecological awareness among citizens and the different administrations.

-To bet on recycling and circular economy.

-Reducing meat consumption and food waste.

-Consume organic products.

BIBLIOGRAPHY

UNICEF 2020

UN Environment Program. UNEP 2021

Rews Aquae Foundation

The International Climate Adaptation Summit (CAS), January 2021 Pioneering solutions to the climate emergency following the COVID-19 pandemic.

© 2021 Iberdrola, S.A.

-MORAN,J.M.and M.D.MORAN., 1994.Meteorolog y:The atmosphere and the science of weather. Macmillan College Publishing Co.New York.

-KELLY, M., 1996. Weather: Global Warming and the Third World. Univ. of East Anglia, UK.